THE POWER OF FAITH AND POSITIVE THINKING

A Guide To Living A Better Life

Colin R. Moore

The Power of Faith and Positive Thinking

Copyright © 2013 by Colin R. Moore

ISBN 978-0615904528

THE POWER OF FAITH AND POSITIVE THINKING

A Guide To Living A Better Life

Before your birth or existence was ever a thought, God had this day planned in your life.

God wants you to discover that He is all you need every single day. Take it one day at a time and live in the moment, but plan for the future!

I'm thankful for all the people who have shaped my life and helped me learn that I have to have God first in my life at all times. I thank God and you for allowing these truths to be read.

Get all you can get from this book, because it truly has a great purpose for your life.

This book is essential to your growth; it is more important than for you to just skim a few pages and then let life's busy schedule pull you away from it. This is an amazing guide to lead you on a journey toward a better life and relationship with God. You will discover that life is truly what you make it. You will see that God has a plan for your life and with many blessings, favor and success for YOU! This book will help you understand that your mind is powerful. Once you set your plans, goals and dreams, you are well on your way to making them come true! This will change your perspective to see your life clearly, and it will allow you to stress less, worry less and complain less. You will make better choices, and it will get you on track to enjoy your earthly life and eternal life with God.

This book will transform your life. I urge you to read it daily. Set times to do so even if it's only ten minutes a day. Once you begin reading, don't miss a day. Make it your business to always read at a certain time of day or night so that you will stay on track to read. It is worth your time because you want to do better and have more. Get a friend to start reading this the same day as you; this will provide a partner to help you stay accountable for reading. Let's change your life for the best.

Some books you read do nothing for you, but this book will, so take your time to jot down your thoughts and ideas on paper. It will truly change your life. Enjoy this book, and tell your friends, family and co-workers so everyone around you can join with you and grow daily! I pray that you and yours be blessed beyond your biggest dreams. Every day that God woke me up, I prayed that he would guide me in writing this book. I prayed that you will understand that life is so amazing once you start to enjoy it daily! I prayed for you to learn to speak positive words over your life all day long. When we keep God first, he will guide our plans, goals, and dreams. Having God as your guide will make you be more prepared for any opportunity that may come your way. You have to take time to plan your life and not just go with the flow. You must learn to not settle. God has a plan for your life and He wants to have a great relationship with you. You will learn that every day has a blessing in store for you. No more complaining and worrying about what you will do with your life! This book aims to teach you how to take advantage of every opportunity that comes your way.

Trust in the Lord with all your heart and lean not on your own understanding;

In all your ways acknowledge him and he will make your paths straight.

— Proverbs 3:5-6

Prayer is your first step to becoming the person you truly want to be. It's powerful and it makes things happen in your life. Don't let anyone or anything stop you from praying daily, because it gives you peace while you are going through any type of problems or situation. Most of all, it builds your relationship with God and allows you to drop a load on Him so He can take care of it while you enjoy your life. The more you talk to God, the less you worry about the things around you. Do all you can to add daily praying to your life; it's a must-have. Pray for peace, love and to increase in your life. Instead of giving into the everyday stress, give into God and He will guide you out of the storm. It is your time to speak with God. Do you understand how amazing that is? Most people would love to speak to a famous person, but you can't get more famous than to talk to the Most High, Almighty God himself. I know many people who keep checklists of what they pray for and mark off these items as God provides them. You may be stressed out about the task you have to face, but God is with you and you truly do not have to worry about anything at all. God has known your situation long before you did. God is preparing you for greatness and wants to use you to glorify his kingdom. Think about all the other times you called on God in the past and He came through for you! When you realized that God will bless you, you should have never been stressed in the first place. You will realize that your stressful situation did not even affect you the way you thought it would because God made a way for you. God is taking care of us, but sometimes we are so busy, we fail to understand that He has carried us when we were too weak and tired to take another step. Think how far you have come and how far you will go with God leading the way for you. God always has the answers to our problems, which means we should always pray and keep on praising Him for blessing our situation. He knows how you feel and what you are going through this very second. The best part about it is you and I know, for a fact, that He has the answer today, tomorrow and forever. Thank you Lord for telling us not to worry, because you will take care of us!

The best step you can take today is to believe you can accomplish whatever you put your mind to achieve. The power of an idea can change your life. You are one idea away from getting to the place you always dreamed of reaching. Your thoughts are what you will become. If you believe you can be something great, successful or special, you will become that. If you believe you will not be successful, blessed or whatever it may be, guess what you will *not* be? Let the negative thinking go; it does nothing for you or anyone around you. Learn to be positive in every area of your life. Get up in the morning and thank God for waking you up and for giving you everything that you have! You may have some tough trials in your life, and I'm not downplaying those, but with the right attitude, things will start to change in your life almost immediately. Build yourself up daily, hourly and even every half-hour. Why? Because your joy, happiness and peace are at stake. All of us have self-doubt, but aim to be the type of person who can think negative thoughts but combat them with positive thoughts to override the tricks the devil is throwing your way. Believe that you will be taken care of in every area of life. Don't allow the devil to fill your head with fear, doubt, stress or worrying. God says, *Be joyful through it all because through me, you will always be blessed.*

It's a fact God didn't bring you this far to leave you;

Trust, God and keep on praying for a breakthrough.

Consider this prayer when speaking with Him:

> *Lord, I ask you to come into my heart and remove all the self-doubt, fear, and any worrying or complaining. Allow me to be all that you have called me to be. Lord, bless everyone I encounter.*

God will work it out; he will put you in the right place, at the right time, to connect with the right people. If you want to connect with people who truly want to be happy, you do not have to look far. You probably already know them. Find people who have that same interest as you. You may have a friend who always seem to be smiling and in a good mood. These people will help you enjoy life as well.

When your faith is bigger than your fear, you will not be stopped. God will not allow anything to happen to you that is not in His plans for your life. It all will work out for your good. The best way to build a positive way of thinking is to claim what you want to happen in your life every day. Your perception of yourself can make or break you. Stop saying you "hope" and "wish"; start saying, "I know I'm blessed." Do not believe you are still the person you used to be, because once you start to believe you are changing for the best, you are becoming new. You are talented, blessed, successful, a great parent, great friend or role model. You have to see your life as amazing already and getting better and better by the day. Think outside the box.

No one makes you think, do or say anything you don't want to but you. So control yourself by controlling the thoughts you allow to come out your mouth and the ones you act upon. You may not see yourself as a healthy person, nice, beautiful, or a provider, but the truth is that you are all of those and can become much more. Think "I can", "I will" and "I am" instead of "I can't", "I won't" and "I am not." Think positive all day, every day. You deserve to be happy and God wants you to be joyful, to rejoice in Him and know that He will bless you right now this very moment. Guess what? He already has and always will.

Once you just look at how much God is blessing you, you will see that you have so much going for you! Then you can start to enjoy life and everything that's in your life. This is when you can clearly see the blessings of your family, job and that you can get out of the bed with no one's help! Look at the fact that God woke you up today. He didn't have to, but He did. That is because he still has amazing plans for you now and in your future. Stop letting fear, stress, worrying and complaining ruin your day. Celebrate, because you know that with God, victory is already yours. Sit back and compare where you were in the past to where you are today. You are so blessed. I knew this young man who was asking God for a job. He wanted any job just to make a living.

Well, God did deliver, but the young man still found reason to complain. So, he wanted more money. There is nothing wrong with that at all, but complaining about it only hurts you. So, I told him to just praise God for what he already had, and the increase in his pay was just a blessing away. Your faith will show God you are ready for the next big promotion and that you are so thankful for all He has done for you.

Be joyful, happy and know that more favor, victory and blessings are on the way. Just keep trusting God to give you all you need. With time, the young man started to develop a more positive attitude. He began to thank God daily for all his blessings, from the little ones to the big ones. He began to understand the power of faith and positive thinking because he was no longer worried about what may or may not happen. He's just thankful that God is allowing him to be alive. Our God will never fail and He won't fail you either. So hold on; a change is coming.

God knows your problems before you do, so trust and have faith that He will guide you through them. God is going to take you to new levels and they will be better than anything you ever anticipated. Whatever you are speaking, whether good or bad, that is what you are speaking into your future. It is so important from this point on to speak positive about every area of your life. Make it a daily habit. In your times of trouble, just praise and rejoice in God, and that will give you strength to move forward. Your tongue has the power of life and death in it. Choose life and speak life.

You could be worried about your job and need to make more money. Perhaps you are thinking about applying for a new position at your job, but then the doubt seeps in your conscience. You start thinking about how many people are so much better than you at your current position. You suppose that they are probably applying for the same position.

Now you begin to feel that there is no way you will even have a chance. This doubt causes you to feel stuck in your current position. Be aware that this is exactly what the devil wants you to think and feel; He knows if you do not apply for that job, you will miss that blessing and continue to stress over it.

Lazy hands make a man poor,

But diligent hands bring wealth.

— Proverbs 10:4

This is when you should say to yourself, *"No weapon formed against me shall proper and Lord I know you will open doors that no man or devil can close. Lord, you are all I need to get this job, and with you, I will have that new position soon or a better position if that's not the job you want for me."* Say it loud and proud: *"That is my new position and nothing in the world will stop me!"* Start claiming it every single day.

When you pray for something and it transpires, you are excited and overjoyed, but when it does not happen, how do you react? You may get down on yourself, start to stress or may even give up. Don't give in to negativity; stay focused and believe that God's plans for you are so much bigger than your own. That door you wanted open so badly may be left closed because God has a far more superior plan for you. If God would have allowed you to go through that door, you would not have had the opportunity to max out all the blessings He has for you. Your plans might be too small, and what God has for you is so grand that you were scared to even ask for it. Don't ever settle for less; our God can give you anything in this world. Do not limit yourself, because that limits your blessings. You have to dream so big that you even laugh at how impossible it seems. Show God by your faith that you believe everything is possible through Him. So the next time a door is shut or does not open for you, understand that God is showing you that you deserve more. Pray that His will be done in your life. When that happens, you allow God to place you higher, and that makes you become so much more blessed than settling for less than God's best for you. God has unlimited blessings every single day, stored just for you. When an opportunity has met its expiration date, always place yourself in a position to receive greater. Always observe your personal conduct and mindset to help maintain what God has given you. One should expect to receive what they give. When you present yourself with a product of greatness, people respect you as such. When situations occur in life, always reflect on your part in the outcome. Ponder on the steps you are prepared to take to change and improve your situation. If you produce fruit of God's love and excellence and his spirit of excellence no matter what life brings your way, you will always be in a position to be successful.

If you were laid off and you're still looking for a job, stay positive, because your breakthrough is coming. God can take care of you with or without a job. Your faith has to be in God, not your job. Don't stress if you do not have a job; it only makes matters worse. God is preparing you for something great, so keep on moving forward no matter how much the devil attacks you. The devil knows your blessings are coming and he knows they are enormous, so he will do everything in his power to keep you worried or complaining or to get you off track so that you miss your blessing. You are too smart to fall for that. Just praise God, no matter your level of progress. Through praise come blessings. I am not suggesting that you pray just to get blessed, but praying does more than you can ever imagine. It is not how you start or feel; it's about you knowing the truth, and the truth is that God will always make a way for you. If you were married and are now divorced or just had a break up, it may feel like the end of the road, but it's not. That may be another closed chapter in your life.

God has blessed you with gifts and talents;

And it's never too late for you to accomplish the dreams and goals you have.

God is getting you ready for a relationship that will be filled with love, respect, fidelity, trust and everything you prayed for in a relationship.

Never stop believing and praying. I dare you to have faith of a mustard seed, water it daily and watch it grow! You do not have to have big faith right at this moment, because just like an infant has to grow into a man or woman, your faith in God has to grow the same way. It takes time, but you must stand strong in the Word; that is how your faith becomes grown and mature. Nothing in this world is impossible when you allow God to lead the way. You have to believe that God will work it out for you in any situation you may encounter. Put your faith into action. A woman in the Bible said that if she could just touch God, she will be healed. Think about it; a lot of people were touching God but were not healed because they did not have faith that He would deliver. As soon as the woman touched God, she was healed, and God said, *Someone touched me.* There were so many people touching him due to the size of the crowd, but God was only talking about the one whose faith touched Him. That is the power of faith. That is how powerful your faith can be and will be. That woman had faith because she went to God. She could have said, "I'm too sick to be healed, been sick a long time and God won't heal me," but her faith was put into action. With every step you take in your faith, you grow stronger and stronger. Your mindset must be on how amazing God is and has been to you. Do not focus on your circumstance; that is the trick the devil always throws at you. Your faith will bring you through any trial you face. No matter what it is, believe that God will do it for you, but always pray that His Will be done in your life daily. Have a vision of what you want to become and ask God to bless your path and situation. You were born to please God. The more you focus on God, the less you stress about your everyday life. The Word of God has power, and when you speak it over your life, the blessings will overflow. Say it: "God Help me do all that I can't do and I'm nothing without you." Trust God with all your heart, no matter what.

There is nothing stopping you from taking control of your life and moving forward. You cannot wait on times to become amazing before you start to enjoy what God has lined up for you. Believe and know that God has more for you than stressing and struggling every day. You have to have faith that things will not end up like they have started. God is getting ready to bring you out of that stage, but it may not be the way you think God should bring you victory or change. You have to be willing to do whatever it takes to bring victory to your life. That will turn any situation around for the better. You have to be strong-minded to truly make a change. A blind man wanted God to bless him with eyesight. God could have simply told the blind man to open his eyes, and he would have been healed. However, God did not heal him that way. God spit in the clay, rubbed it on the man's eyes and told him that once he washed the clay away, he would have the gift of sight. We all want our blessings to come easily without any true work. People want to lose weight without working out, want to get married without giving up the single life or just want a big blessing with no hard work to get it. You have a purpose and God will show you what it is. You will get what God has for you and much more.

The blessings of the Lord brings wealth,

And he adds no trouble to it.

— Proverbs 10:22

Whatever it is that you want, go for it because when years pass, you will say, *Man, I wish I would have at least put some hard work in to reach my goal or dream.* Life is amazing, and you have to stop the cycle of doing the same thing over and over when you say daily that you hate doing so. You are the only one who can stop doing what you hate doing. Do not let fear of hard work stop you, because God is placing some of those goals or dreams in your mind. Be the person you know you can be. Many people have told me that they would love to do something else but cannot pursue these goals for whatever reasons. When you truly want to do something, you will find a way to get it done. No more excuses! Live on faith and attack the life you have planned for yourself. If you never try, it will never happen. When you do try, you feel like life is worth a million bucks; going after what you want brings joy to your life, while making excuses only drains you. Find a way to use ten minutes or more a day to work out, write, spend time just talking or playing with your kids, or whatever it is that you want but feel you can't have due to a busy lifestyle and lack of time. You deserve to be filled with happiness each and every day, but it starts with what you will do today. Start now and soon you will have what you thought was out of reach.

Are you willing to allow God to work out your everyday problems? Sometimes, we try to handle each situation ourselves, and all God is saying is: *I can take care of it for you if you allow me to.* You have to put prayer on whatever it is that is bothering you. Ask God to help you because you have tried over and over again and always seem to give up. We cannot do anything without God anyway, so why not get smart and allow God to run the show? Do not let the situation drag you down by focusing on it every day. Focus on how God will bless you to overcome your everyday struggles. Be willing to put so much faith in God that you begin to relax and no longer carry the worries around all day. You gave this struggle to God to handle, and He will. If you believe that you will improve and will attack life instead of letting life attack you, your life will start to change for the best. Your life will go in a direction that you actually want and will no longer just go with the flow. You have to go after what you believe and not settle along the way just because it gets tough and fear starts to kick in. You are powerful because God is on your side, not once a week, but every single day. God wants you to be happy and show how good it is to follow Him. Once you let go and let God take control of your life, everything around you will be blessed in the process. Walk by faith and not by sight.

When you choose to honor God with your life, God will reward you for that. You will be more blessed, have more favor, and have more peace in your everyday life. You will not wake up in stress, worry or complaining. You will know that God is going to bless everything you do. You have been waiting all your life to get the blessings you thought you should have had years ago. Well, it is your time to enjoy victory after victory in your life. God said that when you honor Him, He will pour out more blessings than what you have room to receive. Thank God for what you have and for what He already has planned for you. In order for your blessings to roll, you cannot keep repeating the same wrongs over and over.

Stay Focused, Stay Positive and Stay Prayed up!

You're blessed no matter how you feel at this moment!

There comes a point in your life when you just become tired of the outcome you keep getting. You have gifts and talents that God wants you to use. These abilities will help you become the person you want to be. Claim it now that God has already blessed you beyond your wildest dreams. Don't stress if you are not where you want to be, because God is preparing you right now to be in position to handle these amazing blessings that have your name on them. It is never too late to change, no matter how old you are. Your past is the past, and it cannot stop what God has for you. God knows your future is going to be a million times better than your past. The blessings will be coming from every direction. It pays to honor God daily.

Have alone time with God every morning before you start your day. It is necessary because the devil is on attack, attempting to cause you stress or worry about areas of your life where God has already blessed you. Read your Bible in the morning; it's the best time of the day before the world starts to awaken. Proverbs is a great way to seek and acquire wisdom and to become wiser in decision-making. Praise God all throughout your day; this will be the source of your energy. Be kind to people even when they get under your skin and tempt you to say some choice words to them. Be respectful to your spouse or anyone with whom you share a romantic relationship. Love those who throw stones at you; God is still going to bless you despite how crazy jealous ones may act. God is watching your every move. The more good you invest in the world, the more good will come your way. In all areas of life, you will reap what you sow. Be wise and choose to live a life that is pleasing to God, which, in the end, will be pleasing to you as well.

Pray throughout the day and pray daily because prayer will change your circumstances. It builds your strength to the point where you no longer feel the need to worry about how you will pay your bills or when you will get a job because you are standing on the Word of God every day. The devil will try and stress you out from the time you wake up each day until you lay down at night. He wants you to worry about the tasks you may have that day. The devil knows that if he can attack your mind, he can destroy what God has for you. His goal is to cause you to become so fearful that you ignore that inner voice telling you to remain positive. Once you walk in faith, you will know that God has the best for you and wants to see you succeed. By faith, you can tell the world that if it was not for God, you wouldn't have made it. The Bible is where you get the Word of God and fight off negative thoughts that attempt to invade your mind. When a negative thought arises, do not even give it a chance to be spoken from your mouth because those words you are speaking will hurt your future. That is what the devil is counting on, but you will only speak positive things over your life and expect for them to happen. God's Word cannot fail; that is precisely why you must speak the Word of God over your life and all your loved ones. You will get more powerful with each passing day. I know this young man who always thought about how much work he had to do. He always focused on how he did not have enough time to complete this work. I referred him to the book of Proverbs, explaining how it was good for his mind and soul.

"Because you have so little faith. I tell you the truth, if you have faith as small

As a mustard seed, you can say to this mountain, Move from here to there' and it will move.

Nothing will be impossible for you."

— Matthew 17: 20

He started to read them daily and before long, instead of stressing and worrying about the problem, he focused on God to work it all out for his good. He told me, "I'm not going to stress over this job because God has always taken care of me, and I know he still is and still will. I will not fear what may or may not happen. God is in control and He is bigger than any problem I may ever face." God allowed the man to keep his job and earn higher performance scores. God mentions in His Word that we should not worry; He wants us to know that everything will work out for the good of the Lord.

God has already set up big breaks for you, and they will take you to a new and higher level. You many have been stressed about where you are in life and find it difficult to believe that anything better will happen to you or for you. God does not want you to settle in a stagnant place for years when you should only be there for a season. Don't have a limited view on what God will do for you in your life. Just because it has not come to fruition just yet and seems to not be going your way does not mean that you should give up. Never give up on what God has for you. God is too good for you to be upset about your situation every day. Know that He will handle all your problems. Don't ever believe the lies that the devil is throwing at you. God does not have any limits on your life. Pray bold, big prayers. Claim what you want, whether it is a home, car, marriage, or whatever it may be, and believe that it is already yours. God can bless you to increase in every area of your life. It may be hard for you to believe that amazing blessings can happen to you, but they can and will. When you speak these types of big dreams into your future, God makes a way for you to receive them. God is going to give you more than you ever dreamed you would have, but you have to believe that it can happen. Ask God to bless you in all areas of your life, not only in money and the material things, but also in peace, favor, victory and love. Ask God to give you more wisdom, knowledge and understanding. When you started believing, God will bless you to do more than just pay your bills, but even give you enough to be able to bless others in need. Take that step of faith, because no matter how good or bad you may think your life is, it can get so much better with God.

It's true what they say; there is always someone who has it worse than you. There are a million people who would love to change places with you right now this very second, because their lives are so hard in so many ways. When you look at all the things you do not have, it could bring you down. If you look at the things you *do* have and pray about the areas where you want God to bless you, there will not be enough time to stress anymore. It's the small changes that can bring you joy every day. Thank God first thing in the morning, throughout the day and before you go to sleep at night. Thank God on the way to work, on the way to lunch and back home. Your problem is not the problem; it is the way you view the problem. Your situation may be big, but when you stress over it all day, it becomes so much bigger than what it truly is. That will put fear in you, which is not from the Lord. Attack your problem with prayer and with being positive about the possible outcome. You do not have to wait for your situation to turn around for you to be happy.

A generous man will prosper;

He who refreshes others will himself be refreshed.

— Proverbs 11:25

Change your attitude and believe you can handle anything that comes your way with God's help. No problem you face is too big for God. Just rejoice that you have God in your life to take care of anything that will be in your path. No matter how many problems you may have, God is still God, and He will never fail. Stop getting stressed over your job, relationship or child because God will take care of it. With the right attitude, you can enjoy your life today. A problem only makes you stronger if you keep a positive outlook on what will happen in the end. The devil will try his best to get your attitude to become negative or fearful, but see through that. Say, "God, I know you love me and hear all my prayers. God, I know you will bring me through this like you have so many times in past."

Today is the day that you break that negative talk, negative attitude and those negative thoughts. Don't ever say you can't have or can't do something anymore. Ask God to open doors that you never thought could be opened. When a person speaks greatness over his or her life day in and day out while continually praising God, he cannot and will not lose. Something amazing is about to happen to you. Ask God to bless you beyond your limits in a way that you know without a doubt that He did it for you. It starts now with you believing and claiming that this is your time to shine and enjoy your life no matter what has happened to you today or in the past. People say all types of things every day that hinder the future, and they do not even realize it. Don't be that person anymore, because now you know better and will do better. Some people may laugh when they hear you saying, "I'm debt free", "I'm going to praise God every day", "I'm going to get married", "My child will be successful", or "I'm glad to be alive even though I'm not yet where I want to be." God said that the power of life and death is in the tongue. That means that your words can change your life for the best or the worst, depending on what you allow to come out your mouth. I dare you to start saying right now, "I'm blessed, I'm going to live for you Lord, and all my needs are taken care of." With God, there is no need to stress or worry because He will make sure you are well taken care of in all areas of your life. Say it daily: "I'm stress free and thankful for it." Don't allow yourself to complain about anything. I hear people say that they're broke, unhappy, and that nothing good ever happens for them. I have heard some say they can't find a job, never got married and are always stressed. If you say any of that stuff, please stop. You may think it does no harm, but it does. If you choose to say, "I will always have more than enough, I'm living a blessed life, I'm a great parent, I'm a great student, I'm the best at what I do and I can do all things through God who strengthens me," those words will bless your future and those around you. Love yourself by the words that come out of your mouth daily. You can have and be anything you truly put your mind to. It all starts with what comes out of your mouth, even when you are joking. Don't use any defeating words about your situation or life; use words that bring victory, favor and blessings!

Everybody wants to change something in their lives for the best, but how bad they really truly want to will determine if change happens. Wanting to change and doing so is the difference between the same old you and the new and improved you.

Never allow the devil to steal your dreams by stress, worrying or fear! God will open doors no man can close!

I know you can change no matter how many times you have failed. You have to get back up every time. Don't sit in failure for long because success is on the way. For days or months now, you have told yourself that you will do something to better your life and your joy, but every day that you are supposed to start, you somehow find an excuse to not start. It may be starting a workout, looking for a better job, saving money or just going to church more often, but something always comes up. Everybody has done that, but it's those who really take action week in and week out who become successful at what they choose to do. Life can get busy, but life will always be busy, so if you don't start now or very soon, you will keep pushing it off and never become that person you know you can be and really want to be. Ask God to help you stay focused and let His goals become your goals for your life. Set a time and date for when you do what you said you would do. Do not let anything stop you from doing so, no matter what. Work on it daily until you reach your goals. Once you start, it may be difficult, but it will get better. Most of all, it's for you and making yourself happy. Whatever the goals are, you can do it and you will get there, but you have to start now. Cut off the television and devote some time to YOU, because what you want will take an investment of you and your time. For instance, if you wanted to lose weight and become healthier, the only way that happens is if you start to eat better and work out daily. Don't think about it so much; just do it. I have spoken with so many people who love the idea of change, but not so much of what it will take to get from A to B. When you want the results without the work, it is only a dream. That is how a person ends up living a life that is not joyful, but instead so full of stress and complaining. You know you want better and God has better for you, so believe that and take action. You may want to start your own business or write a book, and truth is, you would be amazing at it if you decided to work towards it. Live, and not just to get by anymore. If you can invest 40 hours a week into a job, you can invest ten minutes or more to doing something that makes you happy. This time will add up and you will be the change you have always talked about. With the change will come a better life, better relationships, or best of all, everything around you will get better. Your favorite actor, believe it or not, puts in long hours each day to be the best at what they do, and that is the only reason you keep seeing them on TV. Their work ethic is great because they have no choice if they want to continue getting paid big bucks. You do not have to take a giant step right from the start; baby steps are a thousand times better than doing nothing. Whatever it is, just start and do it daily. In the end, you will love how far you have come and how far you will go. If you live how you truly want, your attitude about yourself will be amazing.

It all starts with you. What you believe will always be the key for success in your life. It is so important that you must believe that God will always have more than enough, and you will always be beyond blessed. Take a step on faith and say, "I will be blessed no matter what has happened in my past." God will take care of you no matter what your situation. Your feelings may have you down, but don't allow them to control you.

God is always on Time! Never late or early! No matter what the situation is Trust that God will bless you!

Having a plan for your life is the first step to becoming the person you truly want to be.

Setting goals is the second step. God will direct your plans and goals as you choose to follow Him. You are ready for change in your life and to receive all that God has for you. That is why this book is just for you. No more living an average life! You were born to be successful. Trust, love and faith in God will take you places you never dreamed of. You will love what God has created you to be. So, let's enjoy the ride. Failure is not an option! Excuses are not an option anymore! You will choose to grow as a person, in your career and overall in your life. I know that everyday life duties make you say, *Forget it, I will take what I have whether I like it or not.* You will no longer live that type of life. You have greatness in you, not because I said so, but because God created you for greatness. It is a fact that you will go as far as you believe you can go. With that said, dream like you have never dreamed before. Show God that your faith is big, and you believe that He will do what neither you nor man can. The impossible stands no chance when you put all your trust into God to work it out for you. Your situation or circumstances do not dictate what God can and will do in your life.

God wants to help you reach your goals and take all the opportunity that comes your way. We all have opportunities in life and some are more important than others. You have to be ready for them at any opportunity given moment. They can come in the blink of an eye. Some could even change your life. Stay ready; be like a lion in the jungle waiting for the zebra to get close enough to attack. Darrell Green, an NFL

Hall Of Fame Defensive Back said, "You have to be ready at all times because you don't control when your opportunity comes, but you do control how prepared you will be." Always have your mind set on making the most of what God has given you! No matter what level you are currently on in life, be the best at that level. Ask God to prepare you for whatever may come your way. To prepare for these abundant blessings, begin to focus more on God and less on yourself. Take time to pray daily.

This prayer does not need to be long or structured a certain way, but it is time when you can speak with God with no interruptions. Read proverbs 3:5-6 until the message is ingrained in your conscience. Once you have read it, recite it ten times aloud and mean what you say! That Holy Word allows you to see that God wants to guide you to victory, and he does not want your focus to be on what you think you know, but on his supreme dominion your life. This is when you acknowledge how he has already made a way for you to succeed and be blessed. Write down ten goals you need to accomplish in order to be ready for that blessing. Read these goals every morning and night before you go to sleep. This will allow you to see your goals and view them as "targets." This view is imperative in order to keep steadfast on your objective. To create the life you desire, spend at least 30 minutes to two hours every day preparing. Utilize your leisure time to work toward your goals. Capitalize on any free time before or after work. Pray on your way to work, which gives you extra time to have a conversation with God. No matter how long your drive or walk to work, make half that time God's time. Watch how many great ideas you produce. To expose yourself to more knowledge on your topic, listen to some CD's or an MP3 player that contain information regarding the areas for which you are preparing. Every hour, stop to thank Him for his amazing goodness. Thank Him for providing you all the right ideas and work ethic to succeed. The time you spend on your commute will add up. When you feel like you have run out of words and ideas, speak this prayer: "Lord, I ask that you give me the mindset you want me to have and guide me in whatever direction that you know is best for me. I just want to give you all the glory for blessing me. Amen."

To land a new job, you must put in a great deal of applications to give yourself the best possible chance to get a better job than what you already have. Train your mind to never settle when you are in a place of discontent. If you are not exactly where you want to be, make moves and try to improve daily in every area of your life.

Do not let your current place in life stop you from believing you can reach new levels. Where you are today is just a stepping stone to where you will be in the future. Don't take for granted any day God gives you because it's a gift and an opportunity to move closer to your dreams. Taking time to figure out what you want to be is the start of knowing which direction you will take in life. This is your year to increase in every area of your life. Apply yourself; don't sit back and wait for things to go your way.

Start working hard today and start expecting to be blessed. You are the owner and CEO of you, so why not work as hard as you can every day knowing that better blessings are on the way? You may be in a place in your life where you are not as focused as you should be, perhaps because you are just tried of trying. You have to transform your attitude and see yourself going to the top.

"Have faith in God," Jesus answered. "I tell you the truth, if anyone says to this mountain, "Go, throw yourself into the sea', and does not doubt in his heart but believes that what he says will happen, it will be done for him. Therefore I tell you whatever you ask for in prayer, believe that you have received it and it will be yours.

— Mark 11:22-24

You already possess the tools you need to move up in life, but if you don't believe it, that doubt will hinder your efforts at improvement. You already know what you want out of life, so pursue it vigorously and refrain from listening to people who attempt to get in the way of you reaching your goals. Stay self-motivated and have self-discipline to stay on track, because at times, you will be tested. Some people will not care about you, and others do not want you excel past their mediocre levels in life. Not everyone is meant to hear your plans and the blessings God bestows on you throughout this journey. Stop believing that everyone who shows you kindness is really out for your best interest. Not everyone is authentic. Sometimes even your family, friends and co-workers are the leading sources of discouragement, but that is okay because you are in control of your plans. Find positive, genuine people to share and help build your ideas.

Distance yourself from those who constantly complain or focus on frivolous drama. Avoid those who always try to elicit sympathy from you. You do not have to make it known that they are simply too negative to be in your company. Focus instead on nurturing the relationships you have with those who always provide words of encouragement and truly mean it when they offer to assist you. Understand that those who tell you that you will never make it are simply lacking the capability to dream as grand as you do. They cannot fathom amazing things happening to anyone, let alone themselves. Don't even share anymore of your plans with these people; let them see your vision when it materializes.

Align yourself with people who are already putting similar goals to action. Stay clear of the people who always bring you down or make you start doubting yourself. These people are dream killers. Do not give them power. You will be blessed at your aspirations with a great deal of focus and determination.

There is nothing stopping you from achieving. Get up and put a plan together to have the things in life you really desire. Stop living that average life when you know deep down inside that you can do better and have better. Believe in yourself, because if you don't, who will? Greatness is in you. You can have whatever you choose. Once you believe it, you will plan goals for achievement. Don't spend your life wishing it will get better when you are not doing anything to change it. Have faith in God that He will lead your life to the path that will bring you victory and favor. Trust me; God will make a way out of no way for you. Opportunities are in your face right now, but you have to start being more diligent now. Stay focused. Life will try to make you feel like it will never happen, but it will and it's coming your way. Choose to go after your dream.

Many people today miss so many opportunities because they are lazy instead of doing what it takes to be prepared for a great moment. They worry every day about problems they have created but are scared to change these glitches into something great. Don't wait; today is a new day for you to take a step toward the life you want. Don't be that person who wants the good life but is not willing to work for it. Face it; you probably have to work to make a living anyway, so be the best since you have to provide for you and your family. If you hate what you are doing at this moment, realize you are not living to your full potential. Those who are in discontent with what they do and want to change, but give every excuse as to why they do not try to live better lives, are wasting valuable time. This is bad for your health and bad for your family, because most of the time, those people bring those negative attitudes home to their kids, spouses and even friends. Don't let this be you. Get motivated to become that person you see yourself being with a little hard work. You have to attack life or life will attack you. Instead of complaining and worrying, take action and start setting goals for your life. Have a vision of who you will be one day soon. If you don't set goals today, how will you know where you are trying to go in life? Take advantage of what you have right now. It may be that your job has classes for you to take to advance in the company. Take them; it looks good for you and if you ever were to leave that job, you would take that knowledge with you. Advance your career in any way possible.

Those are great opportunities people miss every day. Instead, we still complain about how hard life is when we can change the hardships if we apply ourselves. Once a person takes advantage of what his workplace has to offer, for some reason, that person seems happier. It is because they have accomplished something that will help them in life. Stay focused and you can have everything you want with hard work and being smart.

Set a schedule of the necessary steps that will lead you to your goal. These should be daily as well as cumulative steps to keep you progressing. Once you start executing your steps, your motivation will continue to increase because with each step, you will move closer to your goal. Have a deadline for each step and stick to it.

Blessed is the man who finds wisdom,

the man who gains understanding.

— Proverbs 3:13

Display your steps in a place where they will be visual cues as you navigate through your daily routine. You want these visual reminders to serve as fuel to keep your momentum. It is easy to get discouraged, but keep in mind that you are making a new life for yourself. Set a time for each day of what you will do and how long you will spend doing it. Another way to stay inspired is to know the reason why you wake up every day feeling like this must be done. Perhaps it has been your dream for years or your goal is to help someone else. Make your work have meaning and make sure you enjoy doing it. Your work should be a passion, not a chore.

Your mindset is the key to making the most of your opportunity. The mind is the most powerful tool you have on this Earth. Once a man or woman believes they can stay focused, nothing will stop them. You have to have a vision of who you will be in the future. Set goals and have a plan for yourself. Write down your goals today. That's how important goals are to you and your future. A plan will see you through the tough times. Plans allow you to know exactly where you are trying to go.

They keep you in line and give you self-discipline. Have guidelines for what you want done and how you will get it done. To be consistent, work on your plans at a certain time every day. You will be amazed how far a plan will take you in life. Let me give you an example of a plan: When you were born, you did not know anything, but someone showed you through example and action. When it was time to go to school for the first time, you didn't go the 12th grade at five years old, you went to kindergarten first. The plan is for you to learn as you grow and handle more knowledge as you mature. The school system has a plan in place so that you can reach the goal. The goal is to get your diploma, and on the road to getting there, you learn a lot. The school system has you set up to achieve greatness. Just think if the school system did not have a plan or goal. We could go to school and start in the 12th grade, then go to 5th grade if we wanted to and the 9th grade after that. See, my point to you is you need a plan and goals so you won't do yourself a disservice and miss out on great opportunities. The goals give you something to strive for while attacking your plan. My goal for you is to not miss an opportunity anymore. My wish is that you are no longer content with just hoping things will change; you are putting action into your life. It will change for the best. Once you believe in the ability that God gave you, nothing can stop you from reaching your goals. Use what you have and make the best and most of it. God will pour out so many blessings for you for all the hard work you put into living a better life. Greatness is in you and in your future. It starts right now. Change the way you view yourself, the world and your dreams. Stop saying negative things about yourself and your situation because you will start to believe them, which will start you to living that way. Use the best weapon God gave you, which is your MIND! Man believed he could go to the moon, and guess what? He did. You must start believing now! I know you want the change in your life to come right at this moment, and it may, but it takes time, and that's okay as well. Life is not a race; it's a journey.

God is saying don't worry about a thing!

I GOT YOU.

So prepare yourself for the opportunities that are on the way. While you are waiting and working as hard as you can, giving all you have every day, know that it's for you and yours. Now you are living a better life overall, so more good blessings will come your way and now you will be ready to jump on them. The wait makes you appreciate the greatness of the blessing. You will be amazed as you watch your hard work pay off. Try not to focus on where you are today and the difficulty of the road ahead of you, because it can cause you to lose focus, complain and stress. Shower your family with even more love while you are improving yourself every day. Enjoy the people who have helped you become the person you are today. Find time to work hard and enjoy family. That will give you a balance while you are waiting. So don't get upset because you have not seen that big opportunity yet. You have to pray through this time of adversity. Pray that God gives you the strength to keep going. Pray for the knowledge and wisdom to grow more as a better man or woman. This will make you improved in every area of your life. Be a blessing to others while you wait on God to bless you with your heart's desire. Show your loved ones that you are so thankful for all that they have done for you and will do. Family and friends are the best blessings in a person's life. God put those people in your life for a reason. God had the insight to know that a journey of this magnitude requires the support of loved ones. God knows the plans for our lives. Enjoy where you are now and embrace where you are going. It's okay if you have missed an opportunity in the past. You may think that you will never get that one again, but I'm here to encourage you to let go of the past and focus on your future, which is brighter than ever. More blessings are on the way, so just keep getting ready for them, because this time, you won't miss out. Do not allow your past mistakes to drag you down and keep you from greatness. You must prepare to be the best the world has ever seen. You will be a story to all. Others will testify on your behalf of how you were once were down and out because you had missed so many opportunities in the past, yet you overcame unscathed. They will tell of how once you put your mind to it, you were able to receive new opportunities and became a new person. When you stop looking at how big the task is and start looking at ways you will overcome, your future is unstoppable. There are going to be so many opportunities coming your way when you move stress and complaining out of the way. Your dreams start to come towards you when you start going towards them. The devil wants you to think about the past all day so that you are too preoccupied to focus on overcoming it. Many people let their past failures bring them so far down that they have no clue who they are anymore. I love the past because that is all it is...the past. Leave it right there and move on. It may be easier said than done, but pray about it. I truly love the present; all we have on any given day is the moment. That is the best gift ever to all mankind. The amazing thing about the present is that in that moment, you have time to plan and set goals for a successful and amazing future ahead of you. It is coming faster than you think. So hold onto life; it's going to be a great ride from this point on. I want you to realize that you have to believe in yourself and push those fears away, because fear is what stops most people from reaching their goals.

Ask and it will be given to you; seek and you will find;

Knock and the door will be opened to you.

— Matthew 7

Fear makes people miss out on their blessings. Don't allow fear to be a part of your life. I know you may get scared, but do not let it stop you from becoming a better person. Live the life you always dreamed and imagined. Your dreams should overpower fear, not the other way around. Hard work pays off; the Bible tells us so. Hard work will always bring a profit. You know that as well as I do. That is why I'm telling you to work as hard as you can every day. That is what counts and what will make a difference in your life soon. It will take you from living a life that you wished you could change to actually changing it. It will transform you from mediocrity to greatness. You must start with your mind first. So get to work today. Set plans and goals so you can know in which direction you will go. Have a reason for why you want to work hard daily. We may not want to wait on the results, but sometimes waiting is the only thing we can do. So while you are working hard, understand that the greatness you are looking for is not an overnight deal. You already know what your goals are and that means you already have a vision of who you will be in the future. With this being said, enjoy your life no matter what or how you feel. You can change those feelings of sadness, hurt, upset or worry into joy, happiness and faithfulness. Look at the bigger picture at hand, which is that a new YOU is on the way. Improving is the key in life! No one can stop your joy but you. Happiness is a choice, no matter what life is throwing at you. Show God that you are as thankful as ever to be alive today. God knows you want to have a better life and be successful, and He wants that for you as well. God wants you to pray and then believe that what you prayed about will happen. You will receive that blessing in due time. Enjoy life now; don't wait for when you are on top to be happy. You will miss a lot of blessings by only waiting until you are at the top to celebrate. When you write down your plans, you will start to get a clue of what you really want out of life. See, I want you to have a purpose for why you do what you do every day. It should not be just for money, because you can go to work every day, earn lots of money and still be lost in unhappiness. When you know exactly what you want, it makes you feel so fulfilled. It gives your life purpose. A man who knows what he wants always can smile through it all, but a man who has no clue is one who worries, complains and is secretly down and out. This can all start with a plan. Don't just wake up, work, and do it all over again with no purpose. Don't just go through the motions day in and day out without going after what truly makes you happy. Put you plan into action and stick with it. Sometimes you have to revise it as you go. No matter what the world throws at you, God will protect you. For instance, if you are in class or at your job and you know what to do and how to be successful at it, you will excel, but if you have no idea what you are doing nor how to get it done, you will fail. A man once told me that he would never let failure put fear in his heart! He also said that whatever he did in life, he was going to be successful because failure was not, and never has been, an option for him. It all starts with what you believe will happen to you! That is either successful thinking or negative, fearful or stressful thinking, which does you no good at all. We must all have the mindset that *I will be great, I will be successful and I will always come out on top, no matter what it may look like or feel like.*

Commit to the Lord whatever you do,

And your plans will succeed.

— Proverbs 16:3

This man never set small goals; he always dreamed big! Think about it; who wants to live a tough life day in and day out? Your choices in life will bring either stress or blessings into your future, but the decision is all up to you. You control what you do or don't do with your future, so choose to go after what matters to you the most. You are your own best friend; you are with you all day, 24/7. Your mind is either on faith, hope and trust, or complaining, and only one mindset will build you up and bless you and yours. Encourage yourself all day long; being positive is the first step to improvement and success. Make sure you take care of you on a daily basis. Only you can feel your joy or your pain. Others may understand, but they will never know how it really affects you on the inside. It is your choice to be thankful and blessed that God is allowing you to have life. That alone makes me happy.

Take a step back and allow God to work in your life. The question is, how do you stay focused when you are working towards your goal? How do you stay focused when you are still not getting the results you would like from whatever it may be you working towards? Keep trusting God for your breakthrough, because it's on the way and it's so much closer than you think. Tell yourself every day that you will trust God with all your heart and wholeheartedly believe that He will make a way for you. There will be a point where you have been giving it your all and still seem so far from where you want to be. Keep your faith during these times. These are the times when the devil wants you to quit. He knows you are so close to the new you. Do not allow the devil to distract you from achieving your dreams.

You may say things like, *why is this happening to me?* Or, *why can't I get a break?* Truth be told, the devil is just on attack, and you have to press through it. You will get mentally stronger, which will help you stay more positive than negative. This is an automatic win for you. You cannot allow yourself to get so frustrated that you give up. In the end, that mentality will cause you to settle for less. God's blessings for you are unlimited, no matter how bad the situation may look or feel. *Do you have faith in God or in your circumstance?* If you focus on the problem or the situation, you will feel fear, stress and worrying because your focus is not on God who can handle and has handled your problem. There is no need to be fearful at all. You must understand God has a plan for your life and the plan will happen in due time. While waiting, you must start and continue to make better choices in your everyday life. Know that God did not bring you this far to leave you now. As your trust and faith grows, you become a better person overall.

At one point, I was trying to get a scholarship to play college football so that my parents would not have to pay out of pocket or take out a loan. My friend, was in the NFL at the time and knew I wanted to go to college for free. He knew I was feeling so hurt that I hadn't yet received an offer for a scholarship, and he prayed for me. He pulled out his Bible and read from Mark 11:22-24. That is one of my all-time favorite verses in the Bible now. I prayed every night, and I read that verse every day before I left the house to start my day. I received a call from a college coach offering me a scholarship to play football. It did not just happen overnight, but I kept my faith in God by believing in His words and having no doubt that He would deliver. The devil tried to make me doubt and have fear, but I never gave in. See how great, amazing and awesome God is to us! He lets us know that if we believe it, it will happen. Know what you want out of life. I know you think that you *do* know and have it under control, but do you really, truly know what you want from the only life you will have on Earth? Do you know where you would like to work for the next 10, 20, or 30 years? Yes, that is a long time, but those are the questions you must ask yourself, because without knowing, you have no vision. Without a vision for your life, you will never have what you truly want for your life.

Once you understand that life is not waiting on you to get it together, but that God is, your whole life will change for the best. Don't just wake up and go to work, and then come home and do it all over again, only living for the weekend. You are better than that, you deserve better, and with God, you will have better.

Here is a five-step plan to become your best YOU:

1. Prepare a positive mindset to advance.
2. Seek out resources to put a plan into action.
3. Surround yourself with people who are on similar paths to success.
4. Write down your plan. Remember, seeing the plan helps you to make it come true, and it holds you accountable to your plan.
5. Act on the plan to advance while attacking the plan with great force.

For everyone who asks receives; he who seeks finds; and to him who knocks,

The door will be opened.

— Matthew 7:8

God loves you every single day of your life. Your job, spouse or friends should not stop you from believing God has better for you. Don't walk around all day with your head down, complaining about what may or may not happen. You are better than that. You are stronger than that. The problem is that if you do not believe it will happen, it won't happen. Your mind is powerful, and when you start saying, *I will make it*, you will do things that will make that come true. Your mind will focus on ways to make success happen. Whatever you think about the most will end up happening in your life. Never let life put you down so low that you feel there is no hope for yourself. There is always hope. There is always a chance, and once you understand that, you will be unstoppable.

Shanae is a young lady with Big Dreams and with big dreams you have to call on God to get you there. She didn't want to just work at any old job she want to work at Warner Brothers Studios. Shanae applied to Warner Brothers but didn't get accepted. That didn't stop her from dreaming, she applied to the Dr. Phil Show and they did take her in. She was thankful for the new opportunity and when she arrived to the location of her internship she was even more thankful to learn that it was on the Paramount Studios lot. It was then when she realized that God works in mysterious ways, because even though she did not get to intern on the Warner Brothers lot she still was able to intern on another lot which was Paramount's. Now that she had her internship locked in, it was now time for her to write down my goals for the 2013 year, which consisted of 4 things; graduating, moving to Los Angeles, getting a job at Warner Brothers and being on a show with her sister. After she wrote these down, she then created a collage of the four goals and put it as her lock screen on my phone as a constant reminder of what she needed to achieve. Every day since the start of the year she prayed about these four things, and although she did not know how it was going to be happen, she knew that it would be happen because she had faith knowing that God was working behind the scenes on her behalf. Shanae is a firm believer that hard work yields profit so she knew that if God seen her working hard then he would point her in the right direction to accomplish these things. Shanae told her boss her dreams and goals and her boss had a good friend who worked at Warner Brothers and emailed him her resume. Warner Brother asked her to come in for a meeting plus interviews and she left with the job. God is always on Time! If you just hold on to your dreams and goals, God will work it out just for you! God will never lead you wrong!

Katera is a young lady I know who has been living on Faith day by day. She has her college degree but still wasn't making the money she though she deserved. One day it hit her I have a degree and a child and I know God can do the impossible in my life! Some days she felt like God wasn't going to answer her prayers. She would wake up around 3 or 4 a.m. every morning, knelt down in her closet, and asked God to sustain her, because she knew it was a test of her faith and she felt her faith was growing weak. Sometimes you have to do go all out like you have never done before in order to get blessings you have never seen before. Her blessings didn't come over night but God took care of her all through the tough times! Katera didn't give up even when the devil attacked her daily. She would claim it every day saying "I know God has a plan for me" and he surely did. Now Katera is doing great all because she decided to Trust God and not focus on the situation at hand. Through it all Katera has counted on God to handle the situation no matter how stressed or worried she was.

She realized that God allows things to happen to us to strengthen our faith. He closes doors at times so he can be the one to open them.

He knows how much we can bear, and right at the point when we want to throw in the towel, He will step right in!

Made in the USA
Coppell, TX
28 April 2026

76720939R00046